Vladimir Poopin: The Stinky Autocrap by PP Savage
Published by PP Savage
Vladimirpoopinbook.com
Copyright © 2022 PP Savage

For permissions contact: Vladimirpoopinbook@Gmail.com
Cover Design by Emily L. and Chris Hammond
Illustrated by Emily L.
Edited by Grace Baranowski
In-House Editing by Smiles
ISBN: 979-8-9868530-1-7 (Paperback Print)
Printed in USA
First Edition

I would like to give a heartfelt thanks to my neighbors Olga, Viktoriya, and Julian for their valuable and genuine insight during the creation of this book. It would not be the same without the special details you provided. I know the ongoing situation in Ukraine is hard for your family and friends abroad. My hope is that this book can highlight the strength and resolve of the Ukrainian people.

Deep, deep down in a dark, dank sewer, there once lived a Stinky Autocrap named Vladimir Poopin.

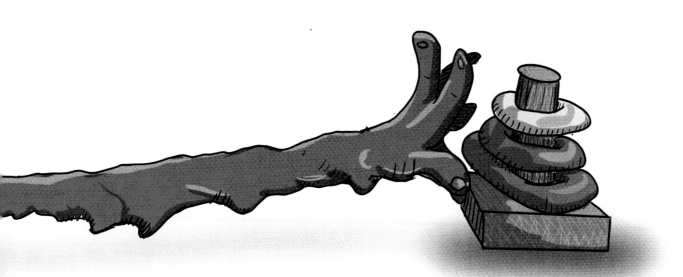

While little girls and boys slept,
Vladimir Poopin would slink around
and steal toys from their rooms.

A brave girl named Olena set out to stop the Poopy Villian.

With the help of her trusty kitty, Goober, and her loyal friends, Olena made a plan to end the Foul Thief's game of plunder.

After the sun went down, Goober stood watch, waiting for Vladimir Poopin to rear his gross, greasy head.

The night got
darker and darker.
Even the moon
was hiding.

But Olena and her friends were ready to defend their own! Carrying their special poop catchers, they climbed into position.

When Vladimir Poopin cracked open the toy chest,
Olena's team sprang into action.

"Catch that turd!" ordered Olena.

The babies swung their poop catchers with all their might.

All of a sudden, Vladimir Poopin
tore toward the door with
Olena's favorite bee!

Just in time, Goober
deftly dumped a dirty
diaper on Vladimir Poopin's
slimy, stinkin' head.

Together, Olena's friends pushed with all their might, trapping Vladimir Poopin under her crib! He squealed and squirmed but couldn't escape the clever trap.

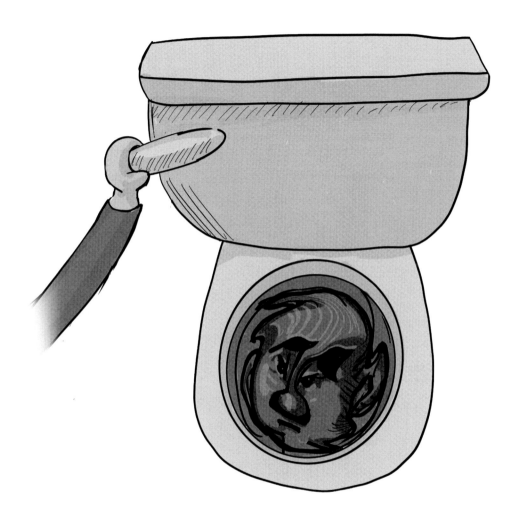

"No stealing from your neighbors!" Olena shouted before flushing Vladimir Poopin forever back to his stinky sewer.

"We can do anything together!"
the friends cheered.

Thankful that her toys were
safe, Olena and Goober
slept until morning.

A portion of the proceeds from this book will be donated to help the families and children displaced by the war in Ukraine. Additionally, you can visit vladimirpoopinbook.com to learn about the vetted non-profit we support. Thank you for your contribution to this important cause.

Slava Ukraine!